Starter Teacher's Resource Book

with Online Audio

Second Edition

Kathryn Escribano

with Caroline Nixon & Michael Tomlinson

CAMBRIDGE
UNIVERSITY PRESS

CAMBRIDGE
UNIVERSITY PRESS

University Printing House, Cambridge CB2 8BS, United Kingdom

Cambridge University Press is part of the University of Cambridge.

It furthers the University's mission by disseminating knowledge in the pursuit of education, learning and research at the highest international levels of excellence.

www.cambridge.org
Information on this title: www.cambridge.org/9781107672208

First published 2014
Reprinted 2016

Printed in Italy by Rotolito Lombarda S.p.A.

A catalogue record for this publication is available from the British Library

ISBN 978-1-107-67220-8 Teacher's Resource Book with Online Audio Starter
ISBN 978-1-107-65986-5 Class Book Starter with CD-ROM
ISBN 978-1-107-69032-5 Teacher's Book Starter
ISBN 978-1-107-64373-4 Class Audio CDs Starter (2 CDs)
ISBN 978-1-107-66022-9 Flashcards Starter (pack of 78)
ISBN 978-1-107-63114-4 Interactive DVD with Teacher's Booklet Starter
ISBN 978-1-107-67694-7 Presentation Plus Starter
ISBN 978-1-107-66603-0 Posters Starter

Additional resources for this publication at www.cambridge.org/kidsbox

Contents

# Introduction

- This Teacher's Resource Book is designed to help you and your pupils make the most of *Kid's Box Starter*. For each unit of the Class Book, you will find two reinforcement worksheets and two extension worksheets. The former are designed to help those pupils who need extra practice whilst the latter are designed to cater for the needs of fast finishers. However, these worksheets not only provide a resource for mixed-ability classes, but also offer material for the rest of the class to use while you work individually with a pupil.

- Reinforcement worksheets 1 and 2 for each unit focus on key vocabulary, as does Extension worksheet 1. Extension worksheet 2 offers further exploitation of the story in each unit. The audio for these activities is to be found online on the *Kid's Box* website. We recommend you use audio to help your pupils get used to a variety of voices.

- There is also a Song worksheet for each unit. These offer a song-based activity, which varies from unit to unit. These worksheets are best done once pupils are familiar with the song. The songs are provided online on the *Kid's Box* website but you can also use the Class Audio CDs. Please note that the audio track numbers refer to the *Kid's Box Starter Teacher's Resource Book Online Audio*. You may like to photocopy and laminate these song worksheets and put them up on the wall as you complete each unit. Then, in future lessons, when you need a gap-filler, you can ask a pupil to point at one of these worksheets and then play/sing that song again.

- There is a page of teaching notes before the worksheets for each unit. These notes include optional follow-up activities which encourage class interaction and add an extra dimension to each worksheet. You may find that one type of follow-up activity works better than another with a particular class, in which case you can use the suggestion as a springboard for adapting other worksheets.

- You may find, according to the particular interests of each pupil, that in one unit he/she needs a reinforcement worksheet whilst in other units, the same pupil can more profitably do an extension worksheet. Fast finishers may want/need to do both reinforcement and extension worksheets.

- Bear in mind that with pupils of this age, fast finishers are not always the pupils who have better understood the new language. Encourage your pupils to take pride in their work rather than rush to finish it. You may want to praise pupils who have done the worksheet particularly carefully in order to make this a model to aspire to.

- You can also use the worksheets as gap-fillers or as alternative activities when, for example, some other activity (a whole-school project, a school trip, a holiday, etc.) has interfered with the normal running of the class.

- You may like to give these worksheets to pupils as they do them or you may like to keep them together to bind them at the end of the term/year. If you decide to do this, you can photocopy the cover pages on pages 54 and 55 of this Teacher's Resource Book.

- In addition, you can use pages 54 and 55 as revision worksheets. Use them as a colour dictation, e.g. *Colour the sofa green* or ask, e.g. *How many robots can you see?*, *Is the dog under the bed or on the bed?*

- You may find it useful to keep a record of the unit worksheets each pupil has completed. To do this, you can photocopy the record sheet on the next page for each unit.

Name	Reinforcement worksheet 1	Reinforcement worksheet 2	Extension worksheet 1	Extension worksheet 2	Song worksheet

 **Teacher's notes**

Reinforcement worksheet 1

- Pupils look at the characters and say their correct names. Pupils then colour in the characters and the backgrounds. They cut them out and use them as bookmarks. See also Extension worksheet 2, *Optional follow-up activity.*

- *Optional follow-up activity:* Pupils work in pairs, A and B. Pupil A lifts up one of the bookmarks and Pupil B says *Hello* to the character, e.g. *Hello, Marie!* Pupils A and B exchange roles.

- *Optional audio activity:* Play the audio (Track 2). As they listen, pupils lift the character who has been named and repeat the greeting.

Key: 1 Hello, Marie! 2 Hello, Monty! 3 Hello, Marie! 4 Hello, Maskman! 5 Hello, Maskman! 6 Hello, Monty!

Reinforcement worksheet 2

- Pupils look at the faces and use their fingers to trace over the example. They then use a pencil to draw the noses. When they have drawn all six, they colour in the faces and add hair. Encourage them to be original!

- *Optional follow-up activity:* Pupils work in pairs, A and B. Pupil A points to a face and Pupil B says the number. Pupils A and B exchange roles.

- As part of your assembly routine, when you count how many pupils are absent, you can draw (or ask a pupil to draw) the number face on the board.

- *Optional audio activity:* Play the audio (Track 3). As they hear a number, pupils find the face and trace over the number with their fingers.

Key: 5, 2, 3, 6, 1, 4.

Extension worksheet 1

- Copy onto thin card for best results. Pupils colour and cut out the birthday scene and the number wheel. Help them cut out the shaded area in the birthday scene. Help pupils fix the number wheel to the back of the card using a split paper fastener. Push this through the cross in the birthday scene and then through the cross in the middle of the number wheel. If it is easier, pupils can use a pencil to make the holes. Say a number. Pupils move the number wheel so that the number is showing. Ask *How old are you?* Pupils answer with the visible number. They then repeat the exercise in pairs.

- *Optional follow-up activity:* Pupils choose a number and move the number wheel accordingly. Say, e.g. *I'm three. If your number is three stand up.* Repeat with other numbers.

Extension worksheet 2

- Pupils look at the pictures. They listen to the story frame by frame (Track 4) and point at the picture that goes with it. As they hear each frame, pupils write the number in the correct picture. Play the audio again so they can follow the story.

Key: 2, 5, 3, 6, 4, 1.

- *Optional follow-up activity:* Pupils can use the characters from Reinforcement worksheet 1. Divide the class into three groups and give each group one of the three cut-out characters. Play the story. Pupils in each group lift their character when their character speaks.

Song worksheet

- Prepare a set of cards in advance. Show one of the owls and ask *How old are you?* Imitate the owl's answer, e.g. *I'm five.* Repeat with another number then give the remaining cards to four pupils and ask them to answer with the age of the owl they are holding. Take the cards back and fix them to the board. One of them should be face down (so that the image is hidden). Point at the hidden owl and ask *How old are you?* Pupils look at the remaining owls. They work out the age of the hidden owl and answer. Pupils sing the song (Track 5), pointing at each answering owl on their worksheets.

- *Optional follow-up activity:* Pupils decorate and cut out the cards. Pupils work in pairs, A and B. Pupil A points to one of the owls and asks *How old are you?* Pupil B answers. Pupils A and B exchange roles.

Reinforcement worksheet 1

 Look, colour and cut.

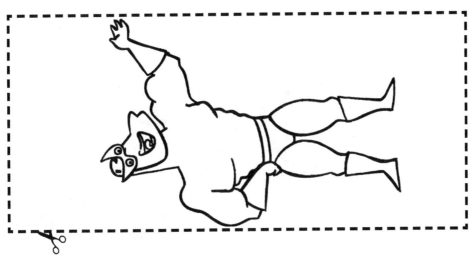

Trace and colour.

Kid's Box Teacher's Resource Book Starter   © Cambridge University Press 2014   **PHOTOCOPIABLE**

Extension worksheet 1

  Make and play.

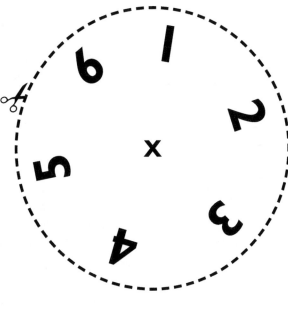

© Cambridge University Press 2014 Kid's Box Teacher's Resource Book Starter

Extension worksheet 2

  Listen, point and write.

Kid's Box Teacher's Resource Book Starter © Cambridge University Press 2014 **PHOTOCOPIABLE**

Song worksheet

   Play, point and sing.

© Cambridge University Press 2014   Kid's Box Teacher's Resource Book Starter   11

Reinforcement worksheet 1

- Pupils decorate and colour the bag. Encourage them to be creative and to use different patterns and colours. Pupils cut out the bag. Show them how to fold over the flap to make a pocket. Use staples or sticky tape to fasten the sides of the flap into place, being careful to leave a space at the top for pupils to insert the objects. Pupils colour the flap. Pupils then colour and cut out the objects and put them into the pocket.

- Pupils work in pairs, A and B. Pupil A names one of the objects and Pupil B puts it into the pocket. Pupils A and B exchange roles.

- *Optional follow-up activity:* Pupils work in small groups. The rest of the group close their eyes, while Pupil A puts only four objects into the pocket. The other pupils must guess which object is missing and lay their guess on the desk hidden under their hand. Pupil A names each object as he/she takes it out. If a pupil has the named object under his/her hand, he/she is 'out'. The winner is the pupil whose object is not named.

- *Optional audio activity:* Pupils listen to the audio (Track 6). Pupils place the objects in the pocket as they are named. Check they are doing this correctly.

Key: pencil, book, chair, eraser, table.

Reinforcement worksheet 2

- Pupils look at the classroom scene and count how many pictures there are of each object. Guide pupils through the example by getting them to find and circle all five pencils. They write the numbers in the boxes. Pupils then colour in the scene.

- Pupils work in pairs, A and B. Pupil A says a number and Pupil B says the name of the corresponding object(s). Pupils A and B exchange roles.

- *Optional follow-up activity:* Pupils work in small groups. One pupil asks *What's this?* and starts to draw one of the classroom objects. The first to guess the correct object is the next to draw. To extend this activity, Pupil A gives his/her picture to another member of the group and asks *Where's this?* Pupil B points to the object on the worksheet.

- *Optional audio activity:* Pupils listen to the audio (Track 7) and check their answers.

Key: 5 pencils, 4 books, 3 erasers, 6 bags, 2 tables, 6 chairs.

Extension worksheet 1

- Copy onto thin card for best results. Pupils colour and cut out the spinner. Help them make a hole in the centre of the spinner and show them how to push a pencil through it. Demonstrate how to play "Spin the spinner" by doing the action that the spinner lands on. Pupils spin their spinners and do the actions. They can record their game in the chart by crossing out a number each time they land on that particular action. Ask pupils which action was first to reach six spins.

- *Optional follow-up activity:* In pairs, both pupils spin their spinners. If the two spinners land on the same action, pupils both name the action and do it together; if different, they each say their action but do not do it.

Extension worksheet 2

- Pupils look at the frames and remember the story. They circle the image they think is missing from each frame. They then listen to the story (Track 8) and check their answers.

Key: 1 A, 2 A, 3 B, 4 A, 5 B, 6 B.

- Check pupils' answers, then ask them to draw in the missing objects.

- *Optional follow-up activity:* Point at frame one. Say *Two ch…* to elicit chairs. Do the same with the objects in the other frames (*three er…, four p…, five b…*). Pupils can also do this in pairs.

Song worksheet

- Prepare a set of cards in advance on thin card for best results. Shuffle the cards. As you show the class each card, give instructions, e.g. *Maskman says stand up!* Then give an instruction without the words *Maskman says.* Whoever carries out the action is eliminated.

- Play the song (Track 9). Pupils join in with the actions.

- *Optional follow-up activity:* Pupils cut out their own sets of cards and play in groups. They take it in turns to give instructions.

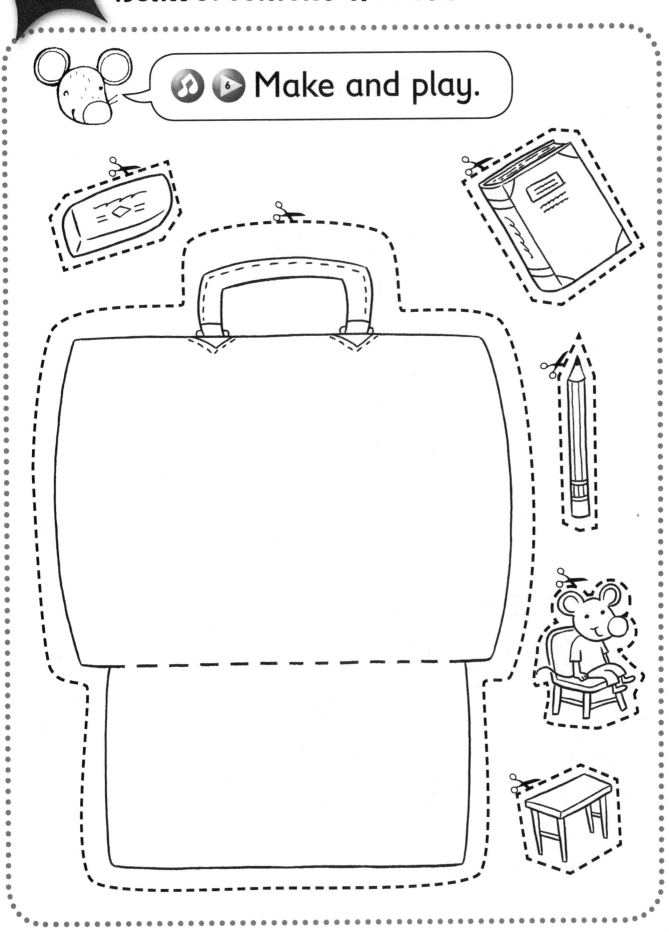

Make and play.

Count. Write the number.

Extension worksheet 1

 Make and play.

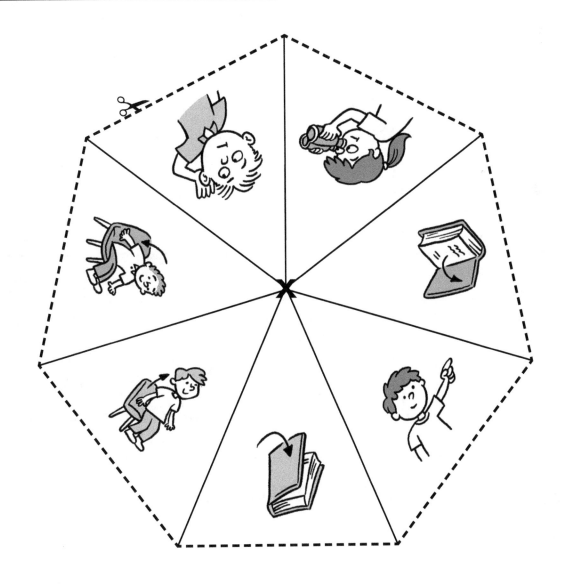						
1 2 3	1 2 3	1 2 3	1 2 3	1 2 3	1 2 3	1 2 3
4 5 6	4 5 6	4 5 6	4 5 6	4 5 6	4 5 6	4 5 6

© Cambridge University Press 2014   Kid's Box Teacher's Resource Book Starter

Unit 2

Extension worksheet 2

Think and circle. Listen.

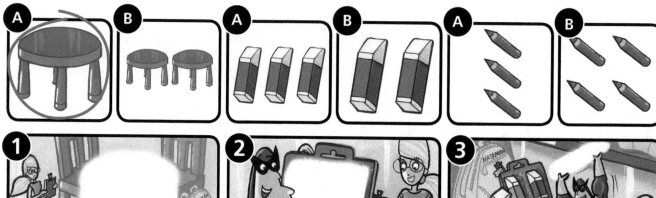

 Think and draw.

Kid's Box Teacher's Resource Book Starter   © Cambridge University Press 2014   PHOTOCOPIABLE

Song worksheet

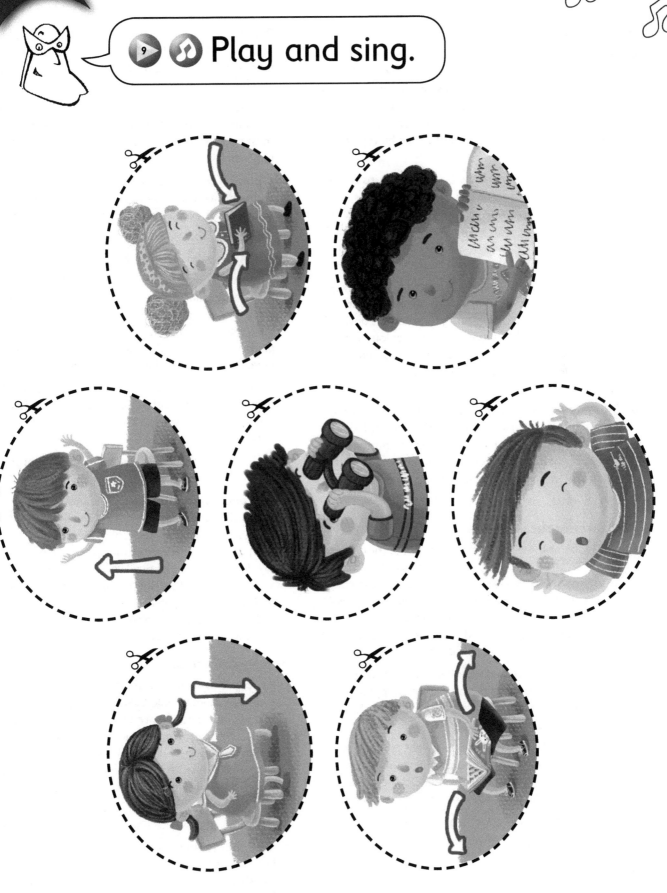

 **Teacher's notes**

Reinforcement worksheet 1

- Copy onto thin card for best results. Pupils colour each paint splash a different colour (*red, white, yellow, brown, black, blue*). They cut out and separate the A cards from the B cards. They lay them face down in rows and then turn over one card from each row to form colour pairs. When they form a pair, e.g. the two blue halves, they name the colour.

- *Optional follow-up activity:* Give pupils strips of A3 paper and ask them to glue the complete splashes to the paper in order of preference, putting their favourite colour at the top and their least favourite at the bottom. Pupils work in pairs, A and B. Pupil A tells Pupil B the order of their colours. Pupil B then does the same.

- To extend this activity, all pupils stand up. A pupil says his/her favourite colour. Pupils who have the same favourite colour, remain standing. The rest sit down. The pupil then says his/her second favourite colour. Again, those who prefer the same colour remain standing and the rest sit down. This continues until all six colours have been named.

- *Optional audio activity:* Alternatively, pupils listen to the audio (Track 10) and colour in the paint splashes. Ask them to lift up each crayon before colouring so you can check they have chosen the right colour. They then continue with the rest of the activity.

Key: blue, black, red, white, yellow, brown.

Reinforcement worksheet 2

- Pupils look at the classroom objects in the thought bubbles at the top of the page. Put flashcards of the six colours on the board. Ask pupils to vote for the colour of each classroom object. Say *What colour is the pencil?* The colour with most votes is used to colour the pencil. Remove this colour flashcard from the board. Continue until pupils have coloured all the classroom objects.

- *Optional follow up activity:* Pupils then draw the objects in each character's transparent shopping bag, following the example, and colour the objects the same colour as in the thought bubbles.

- *Optional audio activity:* Alternatively, pupils listen to the audio (Track 11) and point at each object as it is named. Ask *What colour is the pencil?* Do the same for the other objects. Pupils decide, and colour the objects.

Key: pencil, bag, eraser, book, chair, table.

Extension worksheet 1

- Copy onto thin card for best results. Pupils colour each oval with one of the colours from the unit, then cut them out. They lay the strips one on top of the other and use a split paper fastener to join them together to make a fan.

- Pupils work in pairs, A and B. Pupil A asks Pupil B *What your favourite colour?* Pupil B separates out the colour from the fan and says *My favourite colour's ... .* Pupils A and B exchange roles.

- In groups, one pupil asks the pupil on his/her left *What your favourite colour?* When he/she answers, all the pupil must separate out the colour. Play continues until all th pupils have asked and answered.

- *Optional follow-up activity:* Pupils use a sheet of p and their favourite colours to design a class flag. Show the class the completed flags and ask them to guess whose each flag is.

Extension worksheet 2

- Do a colour dictation. Say *Colour number one, blue!* Pu colour the paint splash on paintbrush 1, blue. Do the same with 2 – red, 3 – black, 4 – white, 5 – brown an 6 – yellow. Pupils then use this code to colour in the picture at the bottom of the page. Explain that post boxes are red in the United Kingdom.

- Pupils listen to the story (Track 12) and tick the box below each paintbrush if that colour is mentioned in the story. They listen to the story again and check the answers.

Key: There should be ticks below every paintbrush exce 5 – brown.

- *Optional follow-up activity:* A pupil comes to the fr of the class and closes his/her eyes with the six colour flashcards beside him/her. Count around the class, poir at a pupil for each word of the unit 3 chant. When you say the final *white*, the pupil you are pointing at chooses a flashcard from the front of the class and hides it behi his/her back. The pupil at the front looks at the flashcar and says which one is missing. The pupil with the missir flashcard is next to come to the front.

Song worksheet

- Ask pupils to remember the colour of each object in the song. Ask them to hold their colouring pencil in the air s that you can check before they colour the card for each object. Pupils can also colour the troll cards the same colour to help them remember. Pupils cut out the cards and match the trolls with the objects. As they sing the s (Track 13), they lift the correct troll and object for each verse.

Key: brown chair, white eraser, blue table, red pencil.

- *Optional follow-up activity:* In pairs, pupils play wit both sets of cards. They shuffle and deal the cards and use them to play "Snap". At the same time, both pupil lay a card face up on the desk. When both lay the san card they have to say *Snap!* The first pupil to say *Snap* takes all the cards in the pile. Play continues until a pu has won all the cards.

 Make and play.

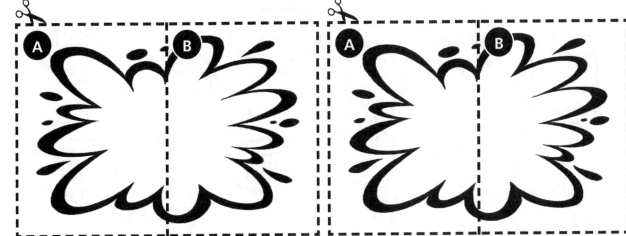

© Cambridge University Press 2014   Kid's Box Teacher's Resource Book Starter

Reinforcement worksheet 2

Think and colour. Draw.

Kid's Box Teacher's Resource Book Starter © Cambridge University Press 2014 **PHOTOCOPIABLE**

✂ 👤 Make and play.

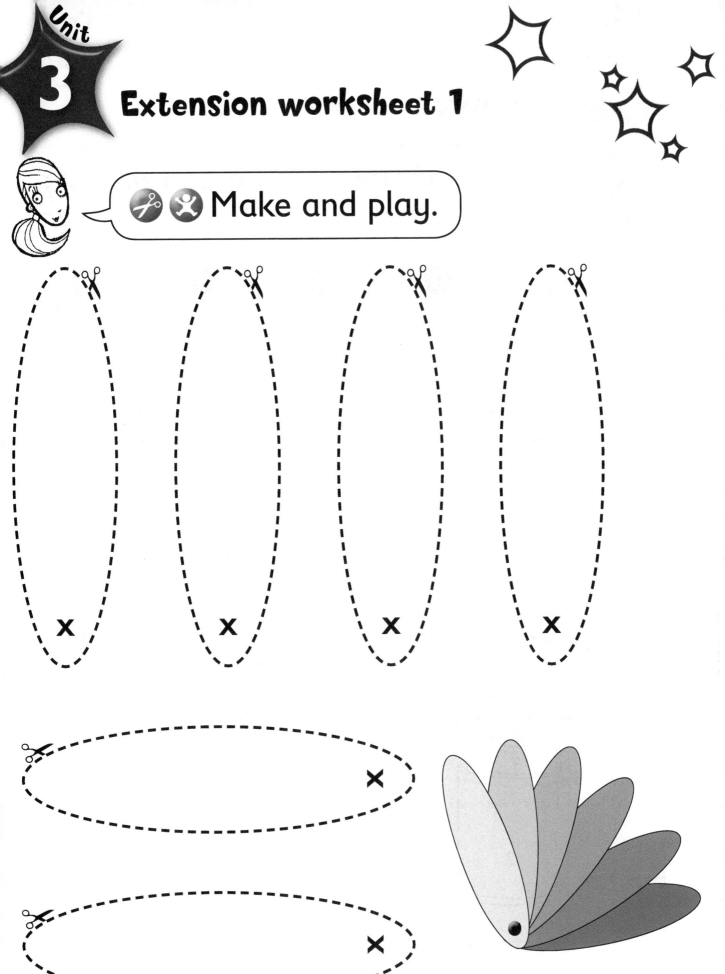

Extension worksheet 2

 Colour. Listen and tick (✓).

Kid's Box Teacher's Resource Book Starter   © Cambridge University Press 2014   PHOTOCOPIABLE

Song worksheet

13 🎵 Think and colour. Sing.

Reinforcement worksheet 1

- Pupils cover the bottom half of the page with their exercise books. They look at the outlines and guess what each object is. Then they uncover the page and use a pencil to follow the dotted lines going from each object to its partner in the scene. They colour in the objects, using one colour for each. When pupils have finished colouring in the toys, do a class survey of which colours were used for which object, e.g. *Hands up if your robot is brown!* and count the number of pupils. Pupils then colour the rest of the scene.

- *Optional follow-up activity:* Alternatively, pupils use modelling putty to make a ball and a robot. They describe what they have made, e.g. *a yellow and brown ball.*

- *Optional audio activity:* Alternatively, pupils follow the dotted lines as the objects are named in the audio (Track 14). Make sure they are all pointing at the right object before they colour them in (with colours of their choice).

Key: bike, doll, car, ball, robot, kite.

Reinforcement worksheet 2

- Copy onto thin card for best results. Do a colour dictation. Ask pupils to look at the spinner and say *Colour the robot yellow,* etc. (see Key below). Continue until pupils have coloured each object correctly.

- Pupils cut out the spinner. Help them push a pencil through the centre. They spin the spinner six times, colouring each numbered section of the kite the colour of the toy that the spinner lands on. E.g. if with the first spin the spinner lands on the car, which is red, they colour section 1 of the kite red, etc. Display the kites. Pupils choose their favourite.

- *Optional follow-up activity:* Decide on an action for each toy, e.g. bouncing the ball, rocking the doll. Pupils work in pairs, A and B. Pupil A spins the spinner and Pupil B does the action. Pupils A and B exchange roles.

- *Optional audio activity:* Pupils listen to the audio (Track 15) and lay that side of the spinner on the desk. Check pupils' answers.

Key: a red car, a yellow robot, a black ball, a blue bike, a brown doll.

Extension worksheet 1

- Pupils colour the scene and the objects. They cut out the objects and use sticky tape on one back edge of each to attach it face down on the scene, wherever they choose, so that the objects are not visible but the pictures can be viewed when lifted.

- Pupils work in pairs, A and B. Pupil A asks Pupil B about his/her own picture saying, e.g. *Where are the pencil and book?* Pupil B lifts a flap and says *They're here* or *They aren't here* depending on where they have stuck their pictures.

- *Optional follow-up activity:* Use toy flashcards. One pupil leaves the room or closes his/her eyes while you place the flashcard somewhere round the room (partly visible). He/she must then find it. As a clue, you and the rest of the pupils must name the object repeatedly, speaking more loudly as the pupil approaches the flashcard and more quietly as he/she moves away.

Extension worksheet 2

- Pupils cut out the frames from the story and place them on a strip of A3 paper in the order they remember. Pupils listen to the story (Track 16) and check their answers. Finally, pupils stick the frames onto the strip in the correct order and colour them in.

Key: 1 F, 2 E, 3 A, 4 C, 5 D, 6 B.

- *Optional follow-up activity:* Say a line from the story to the class. Ask *Monty? Marie? Maskman?* The first student to raise their hand and say which character says the line takes the next turn to say a line.

Song worksheet

- Pupils colour the pictures and cut out the two strips. Help them to cut out the shaded areas in the bottom strip then fold along the lines. They insert the strip with the toys (from the left) and ask, e.g. *Where's my car?* They push the strip to reveal the car and answer *It's here! It's here!* Play the song (Track 17). Pupils sing while they do this again to reveal the doll and the kite.

- *Optional follow-up activity:* Divide the class into two teams. Show pupils the toy flashcards before fixing them face down on the board. Ask *Where's the robot?* A pupil from each team touches the flashcard and says *It's here!* Turn it over to check. Continue with the other toys.

Reinforcement worksheet 1

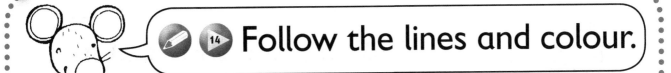 Follow the lines and colour.

© Cambridge University Press 2014   Kid's Box Teacher's Resource Book Starter

Make, play and colour.

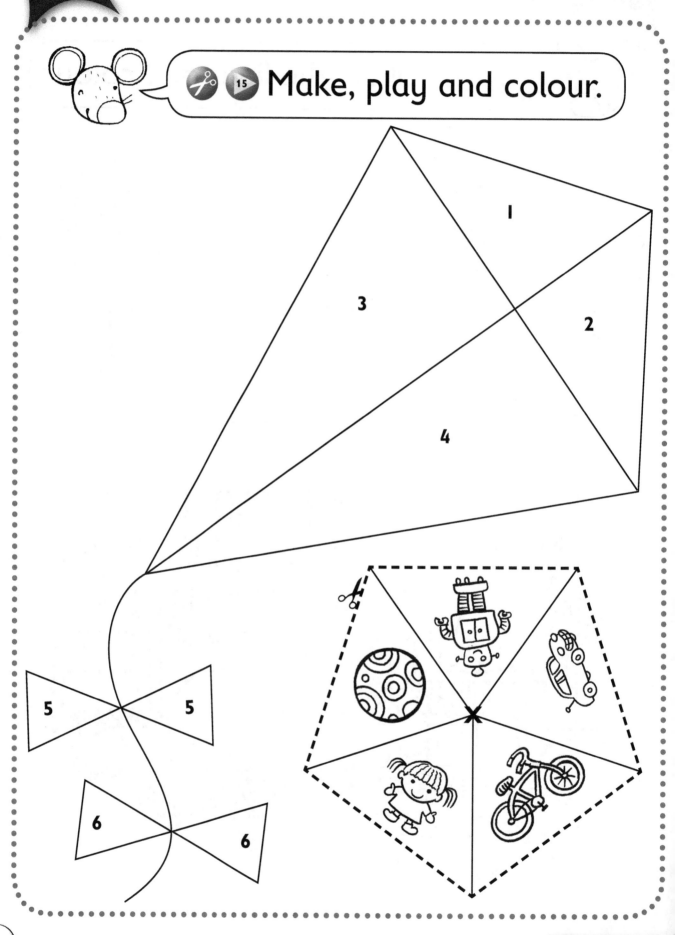

Kid's Box Teacher's Resource Book Starter   © Cambridge University Press 2014   **PHOTOCOPIABLE**

Unit 4

Extension worksheet 1

 ✂ ⚘ Cut, place and play.

© Cambridge University Press 2014   Kid's Box Teacher's Resource Book Starter

Unit 4

Extension worksheet 2

  Cut and order. Listen.

Kid's Box Teacher's Resource Book Starter   © Cambridge University Press 2014

Song worksheet

17 Make and play. Sing.

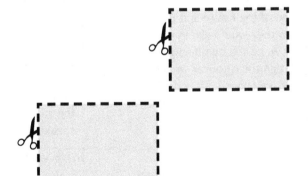

29

Reinforcement worksheet 1

- Pupils look at the pictures and decide (from what each character is wearing and holding) which each character's favourite room is. Explain that the boy in the bathrobe likes the bathroom. Pupils draw lines between the characters and the rooms. Ask pupils to circle the bed in the bedroom, the sofa in the living room and the door in the kitchen. Then they colour the pictures.

- *Optional follow-up activity:* Pupils work in small groups and play "Beetles". Show pupils a dice and draw each face of the dice on the board. Next to each face draw the following pictures: 6 – house, 5 – roof, 4 – door, 3 – window, 2 – chimney, 1 – smoke. Pupils take it in turns to throw the dice and draw that part of the house. They cannot start until they have thrown a six, the chimney needs a roof first and the smoke a chimney first. There are two windows. If a pupil throws a number of a part already drawn (except for the second window), play passes to the next player. The winner is the first to finish the house.

- *Optional audio activity:* Alternatively, pupils listen to the audio (Track 18). They draw lines between the rooms and the characters. They then colour the picture.

Key: bathroom, bedroom, kitchen, living room.

Reinforcement worksheet 2

- Pupils look at the outline of the house and decide how many of each room they would like in it (maximum of six). They write the numbers in the boxes and then they design their houses with the number of rooms they have chosen. They decide how many sofas and beds to put in. Finally, pupils colour their pictures.

- Pupils work in pairs, A and B. They hide their pictures from each other and try to guess how many of each room their partner has drawn. Pupil A names a room and Pupil B guesses the number. If he/she is right, Pupil A says *Yes*, if wrong, *No*. Pupils A and B exchange roles.

- *Optional follow-up activity:* Copy pupils' pictures and make them into books. Ask pupils to flick through the books and decide on a favourite house. The fastest finishers can design the book covers.

- *Optional audio activity:* Alternatively, pupils listen to the audio (Track 19) and copy the number of rooms into the boxes. They then design their own houses.

Key: 3 bathrooms, 4 bedrooms, 1 kitchen, 2 living rooms.

Extension worksheet 1

- Pupils look at the pictograms and work out the meaning of each. They then combine them into sentences and draw the object or character in the correct place.

- Pupils look at the remaining four objects and choose where to draw them. Pupils work in pairs, A and B. They take it in turns to describe where they have drawn the objects.

Key: 1 Maskman in bed in bedroom, 2 book on table in kitchen, 3 Monty under chair in living room.

- *Optional follow-up activity:* Pupils do a survey to find out which are the most popular hiding places. They ask each other, e.g. *Where's the pencil?* and record how many times each room has been chosen.

Extension worksheet 2

- Pupils look at the pictures. They listen to the story frame by frame (Track 20) and point at the picture that goes with it. As they hear each frame, pupils write the number in the correct picture. Play the audio again so they can follow the story.

Key: 6, 1, 5, 4, 2, 3.

- *Optional follow-up activity:* Pupils can use the characters from Reinforcement worksheet 1, Unit 1. Pupils work in groups of three. Each member of the group has one of the three characters. Play the story. Pupils lift their character when he or she speaks.

Song worksheet

- Pupils cut out the three dolls at the bottom of the page. They remember the song and place the dolls in the correct places in the scene. They sing the song (Track 21) and check their answers.

Key: Male doll 1 on the door, Female doll in the bag, Male doll 2 under the bed.

- *Optional follow-up activity:* Pupils work in pairs, A and B. Together, they think of a name for each doll. Pupil A says, e.g. *Nessie is under the bed* and Pupil B places *Nessie* under the bed. Pupils A and B exchange roles.

 Match, colour and circle.

Reinforcement worksheet 2

Think and draw.

Extension worksheet 1

  Look, think and draw.

1

2

3

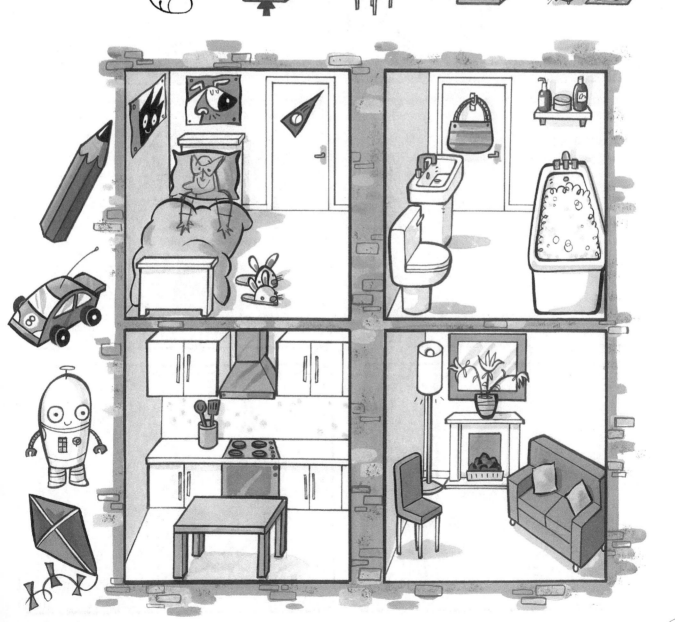

© Cambridge University Press 2014   Kid's Box Teacher's Resource Book Starter

Extension worksheet 2

✏️ 20 Listen, point and write.

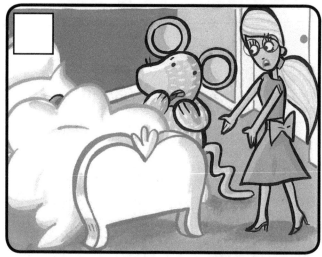

Kid's Box Teacher's Resource Book Starter   © Cambridge University Press 2014   **PHOTOCOPIABLE**

Song worksheet

21 🎵 Cut and place. Sing.

Kid's Box Teacher's Resource Book Starter

Reinforcement worksheet 1

- Pupils look at the pictures at the top of the page. Say a body part, e.g. *mouth*. Pupils point at the correct row. Pupils colour and cut out the pictures below to make playing cards. They then match the cards to form the four characters: boy, girl, robot and monster. Ask pupils to tell you which numbers make up the characters.

Key: boy: 1, 4, 3; girl: 2, 3, 1; monster: 3 ,1, 2; robot: 4, 2, 4.

- *Optional follow-up activity:* Pupils shuffle the head cards and lay them face down in a row. They do the same with the body and leg cards and then play pelmanism, turning over one card from each row to create a character.

- *Optional audio activity:* Alternatively, play the audio (Track 22). Pupils point at the different body parts as they are named. They then colour, cut out and match the body parts and listen to the second audio (Track 23) to check their answers.

Key: Track 22: head, eyes, mouth, legs, arms, hands.

Track 23: boy:1, 4, 3; girl: 2, 3, 1; monster: 3, 1, 2; robot: 4, 2, 4.

Reinforcement worksheet 2

- Show pupils the picture and pre-teach *body*. Pupils colour the body parts in the picture. They use a different colour for each body part. When they have finished, pupils work in pairs, A and B. They guess the colours the other pupil has used. Pupil A says, e.g. *Arm number 1 is blue* (or *blue and yellow*). Pupil B replies *yes* or *no* depending on the colour they have chosen. Pupil A carries on guessing until they have the correct answers. Pupils then swap roles.

- *Optional follow-up activity:* Pupils cut out the body parts. Give them split paper fasteners and show them how to push them through the crosses to make an articulated robot. Pupils can use re-usable putty instead if necessary. They can use their imagination, e.g. put the head for a leg or an arm for a head! If you prefer, pupils can make their robots at home and bring them in to show the rest of the class.

- *Optional audio activity:* Alternatively, pupils listen to the audio (Track 24) and colour the different body parts in the picture as they are named. Remind them to colour each of the body parts a different colour. They then continue with the rest of the activity.

Key: eyes, hands, mouth, head, legs, arms.

Extension worksheet 1

- Pupils look at the sequences of pictures and draw the correct final item in each sequence. Work through the example with pupils, emphasising the intonation of each word to reinforce the sense of a sequence. When they have finished, pupils chant the sequences in pairs.

Key: 1 leg, 2 eye, 3 hand, 4 arm, 5 mouth, 6 head.

- *Optional follow-up activity:* Pupils turn over their worksheets and draw their own sequences with the body parts, then give them to their partners to complete.

Extension worksheet 2

- Pupils look at the pictures and decide who is speaking in each frame. They circle the character, *A* or *B*. Pupils listen to the story (Track 25) and check their answers.

Key: 1 B, 2 A, 3 A, 4 B, 5 B, 6 A.

- *Optional follow-up activity:* In small groups, Pupil A says, e.g. *I've got an arm … .* Pupil B says, e.g. *I've got an arm and a leg … .* Play continues until all six body parts have been named and the next pupil starts again.

Song worksheet

- Pupils look at the body parts and name them (*eyes, arms* and *hands, legs* and *feet, mouths*). They then remember the song and colour the alien's body parts orange and the boy's body parts blue. Pupils compare their answers in pairs, A and B. Pupil A says e.g. *The alien has got three eyes* and Pupil B says, *Yes* or *No*. Pupils A and B exchange roles. They sing the song (Track 26) and check their answers. Pupils then draw a picture of the two friends (alien and boy) in the frame.

Key: Alien: 4 arms, 4 hands, 3 eyes, 2 mouths, 6 legs. Boy: 2 arms, 2 hands, 2 eyes, 1 mouth, 2 legs.

- *Optional follow-up activity:* Play "Beetles" in pairs or small groups (see Reinforcement worksheet 1, Unit 5). Use body parts instead of house parts as follows: 6 – body, 5 – head, 4 – arm, 3 – leg, 2 – eye, 1 – mouth. Pupils add a body part each time they throw a number, to make monsters. They cannot start until they throw a 6. They need a head (5) to be able to draw the eye(s) and mouth(s).

Reinforcement worksheet 1

✄ 22▷ Look, cut and match.

1 **2** **3** **4**

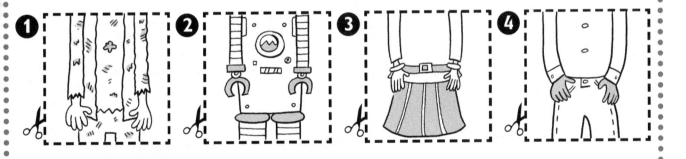

1 **2** **3** **4**

1 **2** **3** **4**

© Cambridge University Press 2014   Kid's Box Teacher's Resource Book Starter

Colour and play.

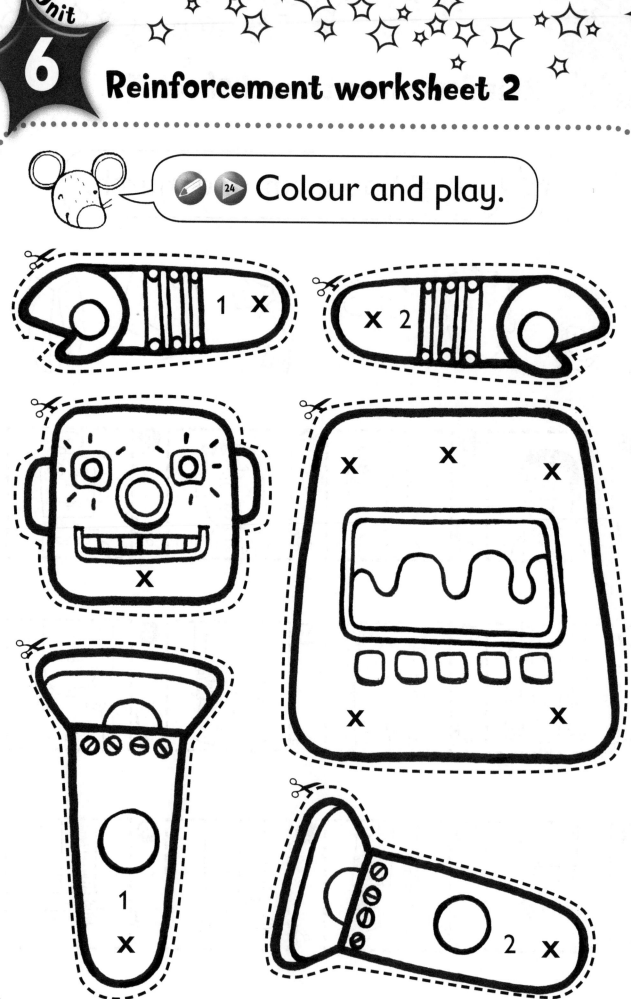

Extension worksheet 1

 Look and complete.

1

2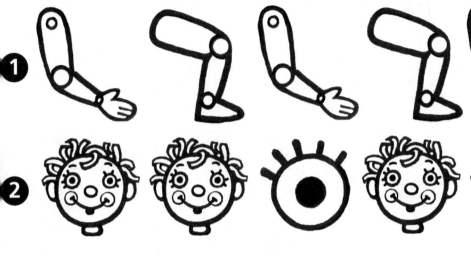

3

4

5

6

Unit 6

Extension worksheet 2

 Look and circle. Listen.

1

A   B

2

A   B

3

A   B

4

A   B

5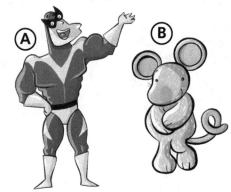

A   B

6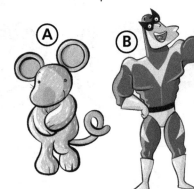

A   B

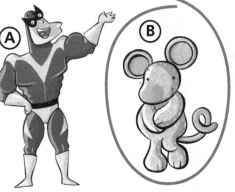

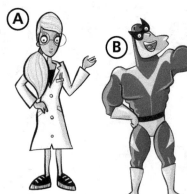

Kid's Box Teacher's Resource Book Starter   © Cambridge University Press 2014   **PHOTOCOPIABLE**

Song worksheet

🔘26 🎵 Colour and draw. Sing.

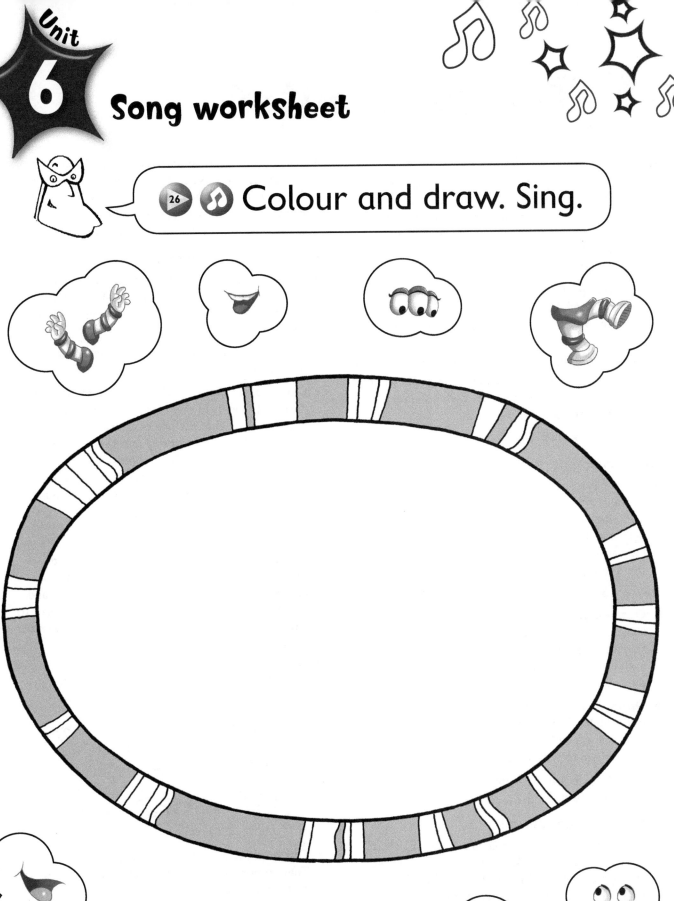

Reinforcement worksheet 1

- Name an animal (*tiger*, *duck*, *frog*, *dog*, *bird*, or *mouse*) and ask pupils to point at the correct trail. Pupils follow the rest of the trails to the hiding places. Pupils then cut out the animals and stick them in the correct hiding places. Finally, ask pupils to draw a fish in the pond.

- *Optional follow-up activity:* Pupils work in pairs, A and B. Pupil A names an animal and Pupil B follows the trail to the hiding place. Pupils A and B exchange roles.

- *Optional audio activity:* Alternatively, pupils listen to the audio (Track 27) and follow the trail from the animal to the hiding place. They then continue with the rest of the activity.

Key: tiger, duck, frog, dog, bird, mouse.

Reinforcement worksheet 2

- Ask pupils to name the animals on the left-hand side and then do a quick survey to see which is the favourite. Say *Hands up if your favourite animal is the tiger!* and do the same with the other animals. Pupils look at the animal heads and draw lines to match them to their bottom halves.

Key: 1 – 5, 2 – 3, 3 – 4, 4 – 6, 5 – 1, 6 – 2.

- *Optional follow-up activity:* Pupils fold along the lines (join *a* to *c*, leaving *b* inside) to create original animals. Check that pupils know the correct name of each animal, then ask them to create the name for the new, folded animal, e.g. *fish tiger* or *figer*.

- *Optional audio activity:* Alternatively, pupils listen to the audio (Track 28) and point at the animal heads as they are mentioned. They then draw lines to match them to their bottom halves.

Key: bird: 3 – 4, fish: 1 – 5, mouse: 2 – 3, duck: 4 – 6, dog: 6 – 2, tiger: 5 – 1.

Extension worksheet 1

- Mime the three actions *fly*, *jump* and *swim* to elicit the vocabulary, then ask pupils to look at the first row of pictures. Say *A frog can swim*, then do the same with *fish* and *duck*. When you say *A doll can't swim*, explain that this one is the odd one out.

- Pupils work through the rows of pictures and circle the odd ones out. To check their answers, pupils work in pairs and take it in turns to say what each thing can and can't do.

Key: 1 doll, 2 tiger, 3 kite, 4 dog, 5 kite.

- *Optional follow-up activity:* Divide the class into four groups and give an animal name to each group: *fish*, *frog*, *duck* and *bird*. Say, e.g. *I can fly*. The pupils from the *duck* and *bird* teams do the action, e.g. flap their wings. Repeat with the other actions.

Extension worksheet 2

- Pupils look at the pictures. They circle the character who is speaking about his/her animal in each frame. Pupils listen to the story (Track 29) and check their answers.

Key: 1 Monty, 2 Monty, 3 Maskman, 4 Maskman, 5 Marie, 6 Marie.

- *Optional follow-up activity:* Shuffle the animal flashcards and hand them face down to one of the pupils. He/she chooses one of the cards and looks at it without letting the other pupils see. He/she then mimes the animal and the rest must guess which animal it is. As they guess, pupils join in with the mime. The cards are reshuffled and another pupil does the mime.

Song worksheet

- Pupils look at the pictures and the actions and complete the chart by circling the correct action for each animal. They sing the song (Track 30) and check their answers. In pairs, they take it in turns to interpret the chart, e.g. *A frog can jump and swim but it can't fly.*

Key:

- *Optional follow-up activity:* Pupils make pictures. They colour and cut out the animals next to the chart and attach them to the scene with reusable putty.

 Look and place the animals.

Reinforcement worksheet 2

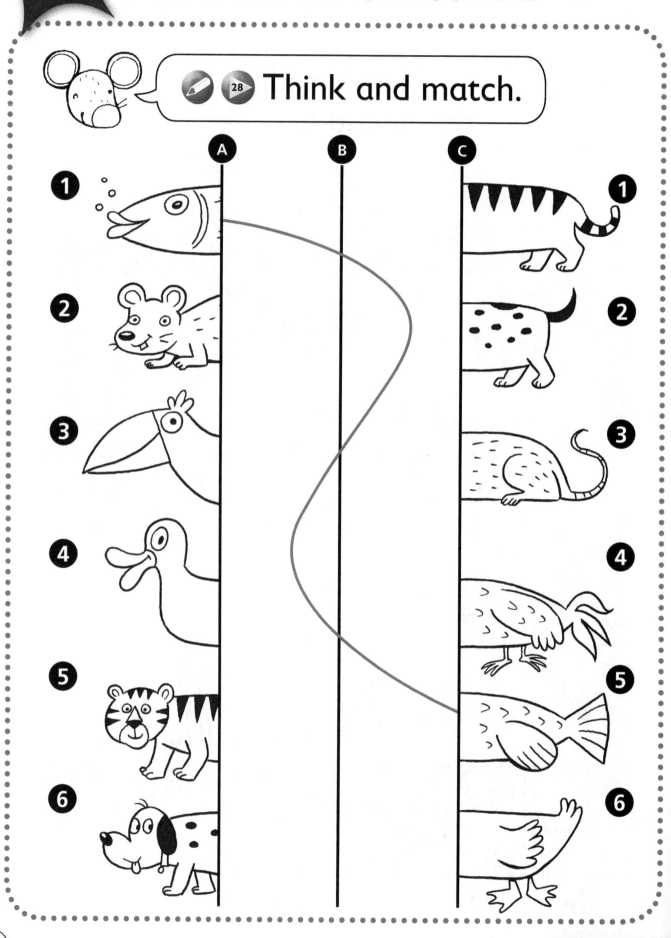

28 Think and match.

Kid's Box Teacher's Resource Book Starter   © Cambridge University Press 2014

PHOTOCOPIABLE

Extension worksheet 1

 🔍✏️ **Look, think and circle.**

1

2

3

4

5

© Cambridge University Press 2014   Kid's Box Teacher's Resource Book Starter

Unit 7

Extension worksheet 2

Look and circle. Listen.

1

2

3

4

5

6

Kid's Box Teacher's Resource Book Starter   © Cambridge University Press 2014   **PHOTOCOPIABLE**

Song worksheet

30 🎵 **Think and circle. Sing.**

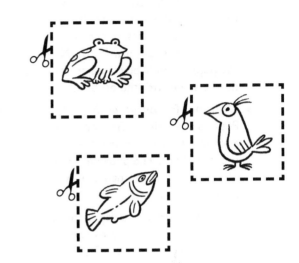

© Cambridge University Press 2014   Kid's Box Teacher's Resource Book Starter

Reinforcement worksheet 1

- Pupils join the dots to draw the foods. When they have finished, they rank each food with an emoticon in the circle next to each picture, e.g. happy face: ☺ if they really like the food, straight face: ☺ if they think it is OK and sad face: ☹ if they don't like it. In groups, or as a class, pupils find out which are the most and least popular foods. Name a food and ask the pupils with happy faces to raise their hands, then do the same with the other faces.

- *Optional follow-up activity:* Use food flashcards. Pupils sit in a circle. Give one pupil a flashcard and ask them to pass it round the circle as you say the unit chant. The pupil who has the flashcard as you finish the chant, names it. Continue with the remaining flashcards.

- *Optional audio activity:* Alternatively, pupils look at the incomplete pictures and join the dots. They then listen to the audio (Track 31). When they hear the food, they point at the correct picture. Then they draw a happy or sad face next to each food to show whether they like or don't like it.

Key: fruit, milk, cake, tomato, eggs, chips.

Reinforcement worksheet 2

- Pupils point at the different foods as you name them. Pupils then use a pencil to follow the lines between the foods at the top and the bottom of the page. Finally, they colour the foods, using the same colours for each pair.

- *Optional follow-up activity:* Pupils work in groups of three. One pupil names a food and the other two must point at that food at the top of the page. They then race each other, following the spaghetti line, to the same food at the bottom of the page.

- *Optional audio activity:* Alternatively, pupils point at the food and follow the spaghetti lines as they listen to the audio (Track 32). They then colour the food.

Key: chips, tomato, milk, fruit, cake, egg.

Extension worksheet 1

- Use one worksheet per group or play as a class. The first pupil names a food, e.g. *eggs* and the pupil on his/her left says *I like eggs* or *I don't like eggs*. If the answer is *I like*, the first pupil colours in a section of the chart next to the correct picture. Pupils continue to ask around the group until the pie chart is complete and they can see which the favourite food is.

- *Optional follow-up activity:* Fix the food flashcards to the board and draw a happy face and a sad face underneath each one. Two pupils come to the front. Name a food, e.g. *milk*. The pupils make a happy face or sad face depending on whether they like or don't like the food. Ask them to say the sentence, for example *I like milk*. Continue with other foods and pupils.

Extension worksheet 2

- Pupils cut out the frames from the story and place them on a strip of A3 paper in the order they remember. Pupils listen to the story (Track 33) and check their answers. Finally, pupils stick the frames onto the strip in the correct order and colour them in.

Key: 1 B, 2 F, 3 C, 4 E, 5 A, 6 D.

- *Optional follow-up activity:* Say a line from the story to the class. Ask *Monty? Marie? Maskman?* The first student to raise their hand and say which character says the line takes the next turn to say a line.

Song worksheet

- Pupils look at the two empty plates. Point at the plate with the happy face and say *I like*; then point at the plate with the sad face and say *I don't like*. Pupils look at the pictograms of the food and draw a line between the food and the plate depending on whether the parrot liked or didn't like the food. Pupils sing the song (Track 34) and check their answers.

Key: Like: tomatoes, fruit, cake, milk.
Don't like: chips, egg.

- *Optional follow-up activity:* Put the six food flashcards on the floor and place an empty plastic bottle on top of each. Give one pupil a ball and ask him/her to roll it towards the bottles. When he/she knocks down a bottle, he/she must say whether he/she likes or doesn't like that food.

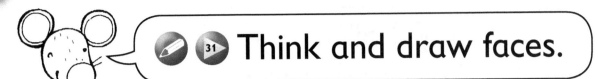

Think and draw faces.

Follow the lines and colour.

Extension worksheet 1

 Ask, answer and colour.

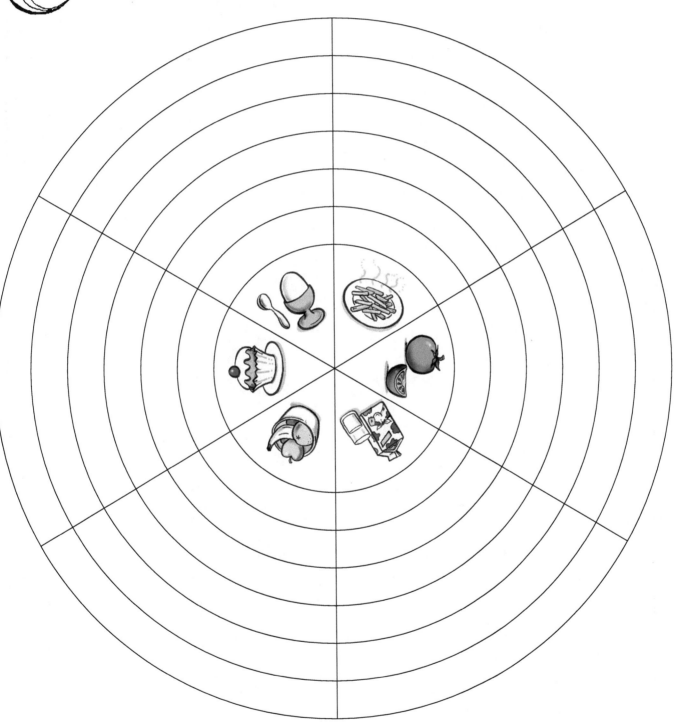

© Cambridge University Press 2014   Kid's Box Teacher's Resource Book Starter

Extension worksheet 2

 Cut and order. Listen.

Song worksheet

   Look and match. Sing.

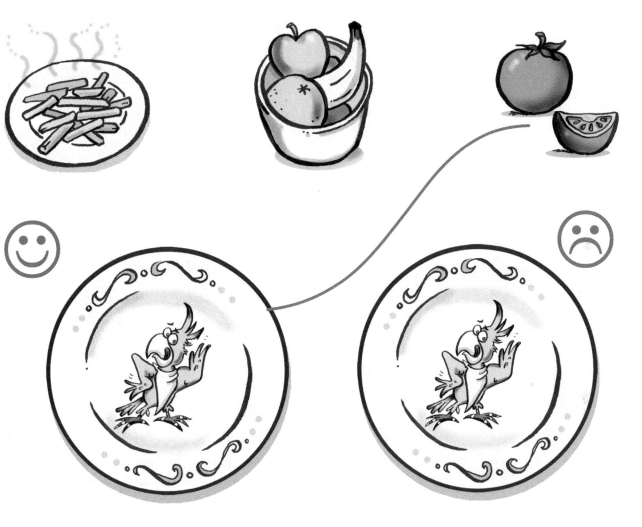

© Cambridge University Press 2014   Kid's Box Teacher's Resource Book Starter   **53**

Hello!

Thanks and acknowledgements

Kathryn Escribano wishes to thank the staff and children at the CP Narciso Alonso Cortés, Valladolid (Spain) on whom the ideas have been tried and tested. She would also like to acknowledge the patience and understanding of her family and friends from whom time was taken to write this book.

The authors and publishers are grateful to the following illustrators:

Melanie Sharp, c/o Sylvie Poggio; Gary Swift; Lisa Williams, c/o Sylvie Poggio; Emily Skinner, c/o Graham-Cameron Illustration; Lisa Smith, c/o Sylvie Poggio; Chris Garbutt, c/o Arena.

The publishers are grateful to the following contributor

Bridget Kelly: editor
Wild Apple Design: book design and page make-up
Lon Chan: cover design
John Green and Tim Woolf, TEFLAudio: audio recordin
Songs written and produced by Robert Lee, Dib Dib Du
Studios